Taking EARTH'S Temperature!

PLANET PROTECTION

Rebecca E. Hirsch

Rourke
Educational Media
rourkeeducationalmedia.com

Before Reading:

Building Academic Vocabulary and Background Knowledge

Before reading a book, it is important to tap into what your child or students already know about the topic. This will help them develop their vocabulary, increase their reading comprehension, and make connections across the curriculum.

1. Look at the cover of the book. What will this book be about?
2. What do you already know about the topic?
3. Let's study the Table of Contents. What will you learn about in the book's chapters?
4. What would you like to learn about this topic? Do you think you might learn about it from this book? Why or why not?
5. Use a reading journal to write about your knowledge of this topic. Record what you already know about the topic and what you hope to learn about the topic.
6. Read the book.
7. In your reading journal, record what you learned about the topic and your response to the book.
8. After reading the book complete the activities below.

Content Area Vocabulary

Read the list. What do these words mean?

absorbs

atmosphere

composting

concentrate

drought

emissions

insulate

satellite

unreliable

vegetation

After Reading:

Comprehension and Extension Activity

After reading the book, work on the following questions with your child or students in order to check their level of reading comprehension and content mastery.

1. How does burning fossil fuels cause Earth to warm? (Summarize)
2. Why are solar power plants often located in deserts? (Infer)
3. Why might a builder choose local materials for a green building? (Asking Questions)
4. What items can you recycle to cut your carbon footprint? (Text to Self Connection)
5. How do bicycling and walking affect your carbon footprint? (Asking Questions)

Extension Activity

Think you'd like a job as a planet protector? Check out some exciting "green jobs" on NASA's website: https://climatekids.nasa.gov/menu/dream/. Make a list of green jobs you might enjoy, or come up with your own ideas based on what you learned in the book. Learn more about any jobs that interest you. You never know where it might lead!

TABLE OF CONTENTS

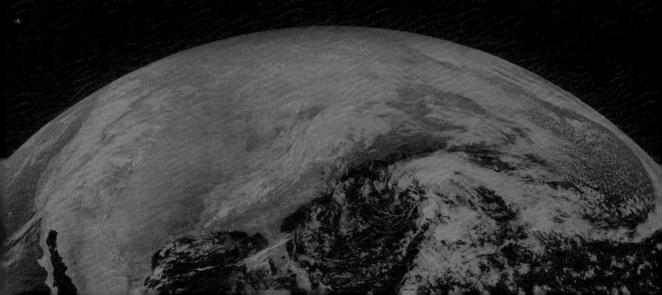

CHAPTER ONE

THE CHANGING CLIMATE

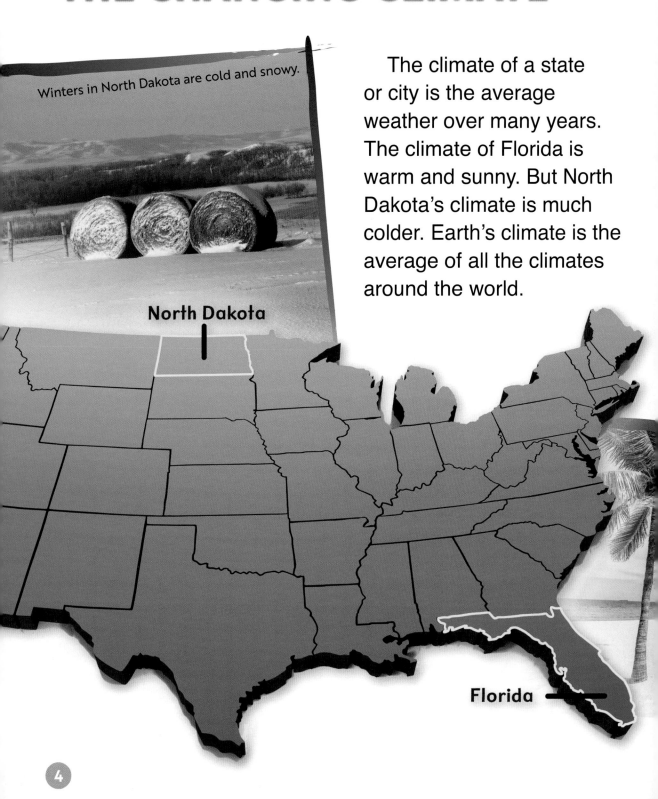

Winters in North Dakota are cold and snowy.

North Dakota

Florida

The climate of a state or city is the average weather over many years. The climate of Florida is warm and sunny. But North Dakota's climate is much colder. Earth's climate is the average of all the climates around the world.

Climate change is a change in the usual climate of a place. It could be a change in the average annual temperature or rainfall of a state or city. Or it could be a change in Earth's average temperature.

Scientists say that Earth's climate is growing warmer. The planet's average temperature has risen by about 1.4 degrees Fahrenheit (0.8 degrees Celsius) over the last hundred years.

Cars that run on gasoline release carbon dioxide through the tailpipe.

A large volcanic eruption can block sunlight, changing the climate.

Some climate change happens naturally. It could be caused by slight changes in Earth's orbit or by the eruption of a large volcano. But most scientists say much of the current warming is caused by rising levels of carbon dioxide in the **atmosphere**. This is very likely caused by the burning of fossil fuels.

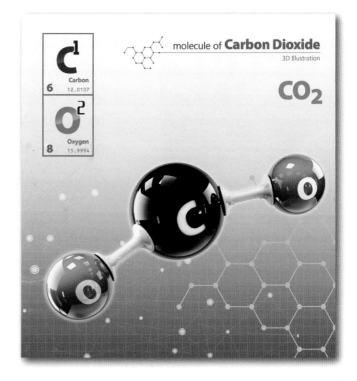

molecule of **Carbon Dioxide**
3D Illustration

C^1
Carbon
6   12.0107

O^2
Oxygen
8   15.9994

CO_2

Scientists around the world try to understand how climate change affects the natural world.

IS CLIMATE CHANGE REAL?

Some people believe climate change is not really happening. Others argue the change is natural and not caused by people. But most scientists disagree. Scientists have understood the basics of climate change for years. They have learned about the climate by observing the natural world, planning experiments, and collecting data. Most scientists agree that the climate is changing and that people are responsible.

Smog hanging over cities is the most familiar and obvious form of air pollution that contributes to global warming.

Greenhouse effect

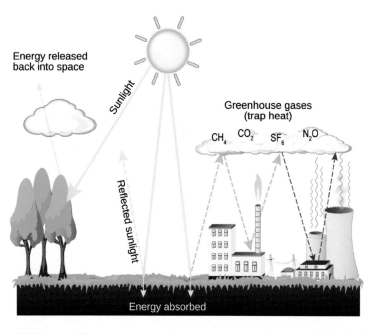

Energy released back into space

Sunlight

Reflected sunlight

Greenhouse gases (trap heat)

CH_4 CO_2 SF_6 N_2O

Energy absorbed

Many factories, power plants, and vehicles run on fossil fuels such as coal and oil. When we burn fossil fuels, carbon dioxide goes into the air. Carbon dioxide is a greenhouse gas, a gas that **absorbs** energy and traps heat from the sun. Although we need some carbon dioxide in the air, too high of an amount is warming the planet. This warming can harm living things, including people.

Carbon dioxide levels in the atmosphere have been rising since the Industrial Revolution.

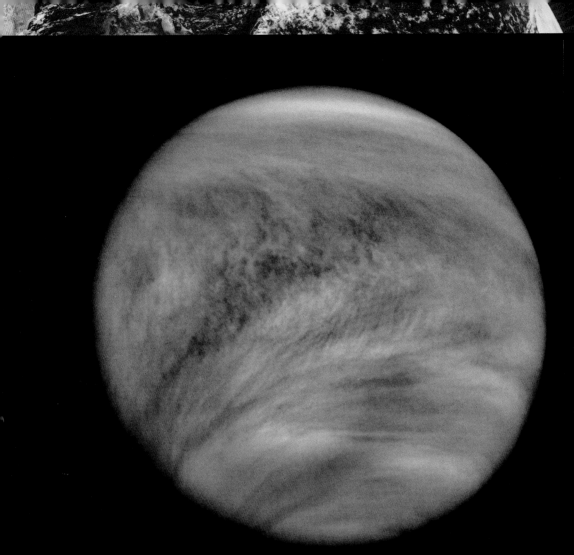

The greenhouse effect on Venus shows what happens when trapping sunlight gets out of control.

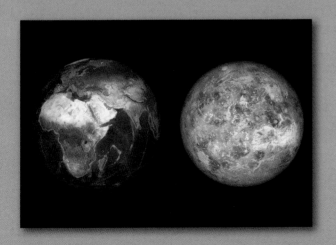

HOT SPOT

Venus is the hottest planet in the solar system. Carbon dioxide helps keep its surface 864 degrees Fahrenheit (462 degrees Celsius). But don't worry! Earth will not become like Venus. The air on Venus is more than 95 percent carbon dioxide, while Earth's is less than one percent.

CHAPTER TWO

WIND AND SUN

One way we can slow climate change is by switching to clean energy, such as wind and solar power. Clean energy sources don't release carbon dioxide into the air. Wind and solar power could meet all the world's energy needs.

This windy mountaintop is a great place to harvest wind energy.

POWERING THE PLANET

The amount of sunlight that strikes Earth in an hour and a half is enough to meet the world's energy needs for a whole year.

We can capture wind energy with wind turbines. These tall towers have blades that spin in the wind and make electricity. Wind turbines can spin any place it is windy, whether on land or over the ocean.

Offshore wind farms capture ocean winds just a few miles from land.

We can capture the sun's energy in a few different ways. Solar panels turn sunlight into electricity directly. Solar thermal plants use mirrors or lenses to **concentrate** heat from the sun, and then use the heat to make electricity.

Solar thermal plants use sunlight to make steam, which powers a turbine and makes electricity.

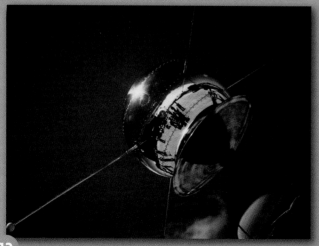

SOLAR SATELLITE

In 1958, the United States (U.S) space program launched Vanguard 1, *the first manmade **satellite** to be powered by solar energy. The oldest satellite still orbiting Earth, it has traveled more than six billion miles (9.7 billion kilometers).*

The Ivanpah solar plant, built in California's Mojave Desert, has been making clean electricity since 2014.

These days, more and more countries, states, and cities are turning to clean energy. The world's largest solar thermal plant is in the Mojave Desert. It makes enough electricity to power 140,000 California homes. The city of Houston, Texas, has built a solar plant that provides ten percent of the city's needs.

The city of Houston uses clean energy to meet 89% of its energy needs.

On wind energy, Denmark is leading the way. The European country plans to be off fossil fuels by 2050. The island of Samso, off the Danish coast, already makes its own electricity from wind. The island makes so much electricity, it sells the extra to the mainland.

Much of Samso Island's energy comes from wind turbines owned by the islanders themselves.

Companies are also switching to clean energy. In 2017 Google powered its offices and data centers with 100 percent wind and solar energy. The Internet company buys more clean energy than any other company in the world.

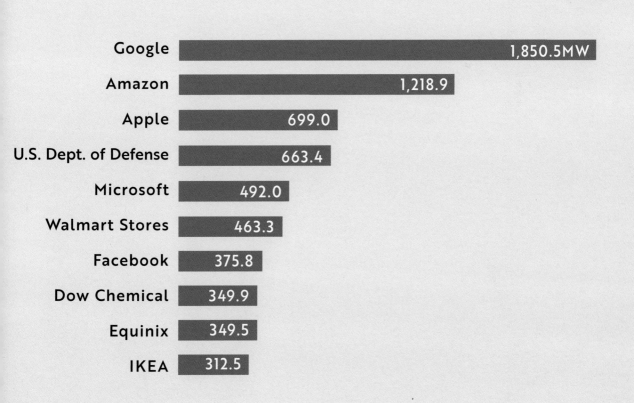

TOP CORPORATE CLEAN-POWER BUYERS

Cumulative U.S. renewable energy

Google	1,850.5MW
Amazon	1,218.9
Apple	699.0
U.S. Dept. of Defense	663.4
Microsoft	492.0
Walmart Stores	463.3
Facebook	375.8
Dow Chemical	349.9
Equinix	349.5
IKEA	312.5

Source: Bloomberg New Energy Finance

Wind and solar power come with challenges. One challenge is **unreliable** weather. Critics point out that the wind doesn't always blow and the sun doesn't always shine. When that happens, we can't make electricity. But as more wind turbines and solar plants are built in more places, reliability improves. The wind is always blowing and the sun is always shining somewhere.

One of the biggest challenges to solar power is unreliable weather. Researchers are studying ways for solar plants to store energy to use on days like this.

Another challenge is high cost. In the past, wind and solar power have been expensive. But as more people make the switch, the price is dropping.

SOLAR USAGE GROWS AS INSTALLATION PRICING FALLS

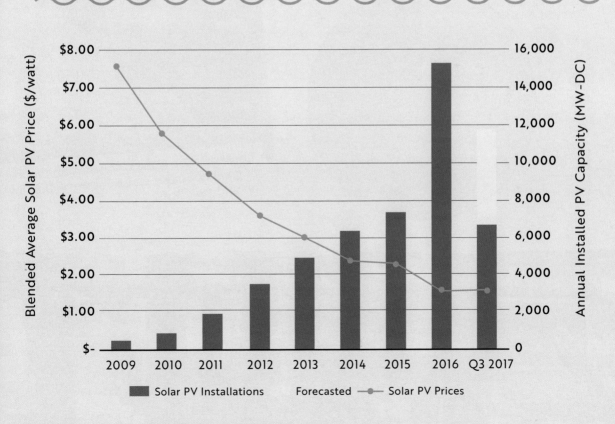

Source: GTM Research, Solar Energy Industries Association

CHAPTER THREE

BETTER BUILDINGS AND CARS

Buildings and vehicles use a lot of energy. In the U.S., buildings make up almost 40 percent of greenhouse gas **emissions**. Transportation, mostly cars and trucks, makes up nearly another 30 percent.

TOTAL U.S. GREENHOUSE GAS EMISSIONS BY ECONOMIC SECTOR IN 2015

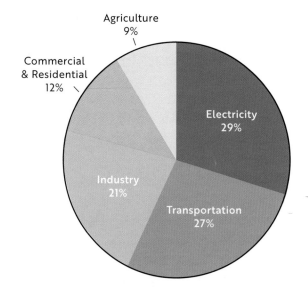

Agriculture 9%

Commercial & Residential 12%

Electricity 29%

Industry 21%

Transportation 27%

Transportation is the second leading source of greenhouse gas emissions in the U.S., just behind electricity.

More and more buildings are going "green." Green buildings use less energy and water than ordinary buildings. Green buildings may be built with local products, so products don't have to be shipped from around the world. They may contain recycled material, like carpets made from recycled plastic bottles.

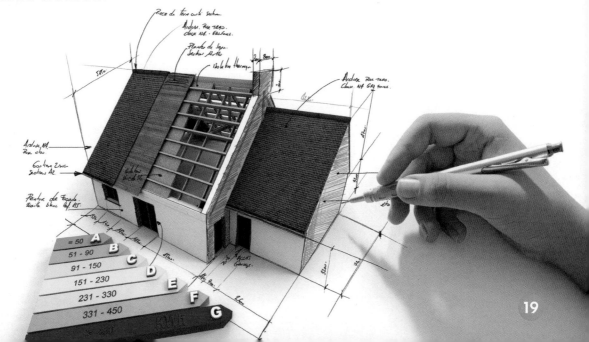

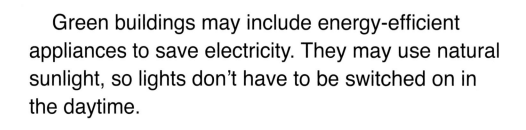

Green buildings may include energy-efficient appliances to save electricity. They may use natural sunlight, so lights don't have to be switched on in the daytime.

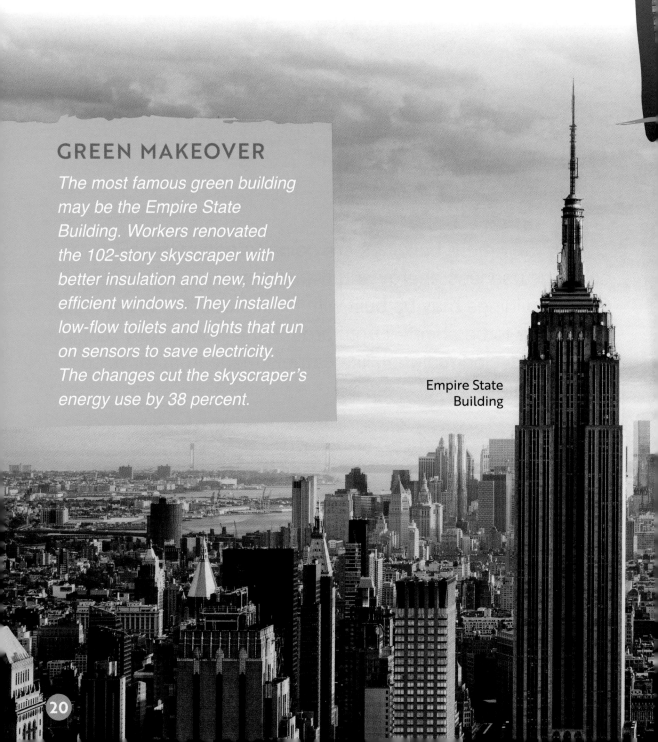

GREEN MAKEOVER

The most famous green building may be the Empire State Building. Workers renovated the 102-story skyscraper with better insulation and new, highly efficient windows. They installed low-flow toilets and lights that run on sensors to save electricity. The changes cut the skyscraper's energy use by 38 percent.

Empire State Building

A roof can make energy (left) or conserve energy by keeping a house cool (right).

Many green buildings have special roofs. A "green roof," planted with wildflowers and other plants, can **insulate** a building and provide a home for animals. Roofs covered with solar panels can make clean electricity. In hot, sunny places, "cool roofs" can reflect sunlight and absorb less heat.

Some housing communities are built to be energy efficient and use clean energy.

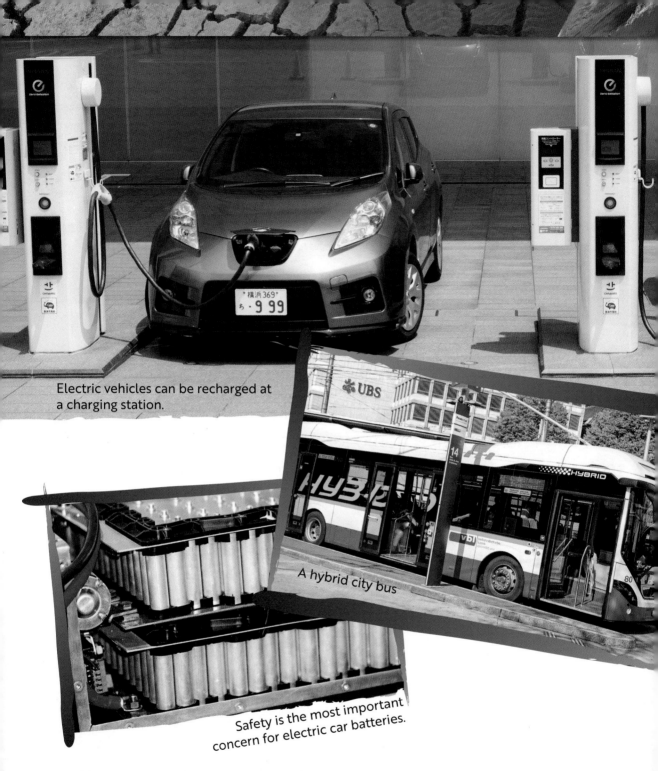

Electric vehicles can be recharged at a charging station.

A hybrid city bus

Safety is the most important concern for electric car batteries.

Transportation can also be made more efficient. Cars and trucks can run on clean power. Electric cars can run on clean electricity that is made from wind or solar power. Hybrid vehicles can run on gasoline or electricity stored in a battery.

Cars release carbon dioxide from their tailpipes.

CALIFORNIA

Cars and trucks sold in California must be very fuel efficient, meaning they must travel farther on a gallon of gasoline. Each gallon of gas saved keeps 20 pounds (9 kilograms) of carbon dioxide out of the air. Thirteen other states and Washington, D.C., follow California's strict standards.

This home with solar roof tiles can get 100% of its energy from the sun.

ROOFTOP POWER PLANT

Two companies, Tesla and Solar City, teamed up to develop solar roof tiles. The tiles look like regular roof tiles, but can make electricity. The electricity can be stored in a battery, and can then be used to power a home and an electric car.

CHAPTER FOUR

GREENING THE PLANET

Forests store huge amounts of carbon dioxide. Trees soak up carbon dioxide from the air as they grow. They release it when they burn or rot.

Burning or cutting down trees feeds climate change. This deforestation happens when people clear forests for farms or to make room for towns and cities. Up to 15 percent of the world's greenhouse gas emissions can come from deforestation.

According to the World Wildlife Fund, about 36 football fields worth of forest are lost every minute.

SHRINKING FORESTS

Forests cover thirty percent of Earth's land. That might sound like a lot, but they are vanishing. An area of forest larger than the state of Mississippi disappears every year.

Mississippi

CARBON STORAGE SYSTEM

Green plants use sunlight, water, and carbon dioxide from the air to make food for themselves. Plants absorb carbon dioxide through their leaves. Cover a leaf on a living plant with petroleum jelly. The jelly allows sunlight to pass through but prevents the leaf from soaking up carbon dioxide. Check the leaf after a few days. What happens?

One way to slow climate change is to prevent deforestation. Trees can be replanted to replace the ones that have been cut down.

Planting trees to replace areas of forests that have been damaged is a practice known as reforestation.

SUPER SOAKERS

Old trees in a forest soak up more carbon dioxide than young trees. Scientists have discovered that old trees grow the fastest. The biggest, oldest trees can put on 1,300 pounds (590 kilograms) of wood, bark, and leaves in a single year.

The Forest Stewardship Council promotes wood and paper from forests where trees are replanted. The products come with an FSC label, so people can know what they are buying.

In addition to benefiting climate change, planting trees also protects soil and water quality.

Planting trees in new places can also slow climate change. In Africa, 11 countries are building the Great Green Wall.

The Great Green Wall gives people a way to restore land that has been damaged by human activity.

This belt of trees, shrubs, and other plants will be 4,381 miles (7050.5 kilometers) long and will span the entire width of Africa. The country of Senegal is leading the way. People there have planted two million trees a year every year since 2008.

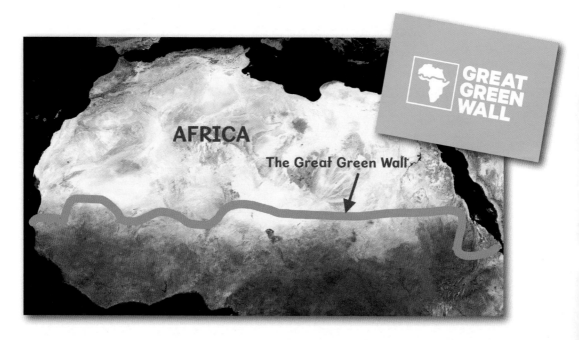

AFRICA

The Great Green Wall

GREAT GREEN WALL

Permafrost occurs in areas where temperatures rarely rise above freezing.

In chilly northern Russia, people are trying something else. The ground there is permafrost, permanently frozen ground. The remains of **vegetation** are locked in the frozen soil. As the climate warms, the frozen ground could thaw. The vegetation could rot and release carbon dioxide into the air.

To prevent the permafrost from thawing, scientists are bringing in reindeer and other large animals. The animals trample the snow. Without animals, snow acts like a blanket, keeping the ground from freezing. But trampled snow doesn't insulate as well, so the ground stays colder. The scientists are testing whether the animals can help keep the ground frozen. If so, they can keep carbon dioxide locked safely in the ground.

CHAPTER FIVE

LIFE ON A CHANGING PLANET

As the climate warms, the world is changing. People are finding ways to adjust to the effects of climate change.

Muir Glacier, Alaska

August 13, 1941

August 31, 2004

Homes near the coasts are at risk from rising seas.

Sea ice that forms from sea water does not raise the level of the sea if it melts, unlike melting ice sheets.

One of the biggest changes is sea level rise. As the climate warms, huge sheets of ice that sit on places like Greenland and Antarctica are melting. These ice sheets are crumbling into the sea. The melting ice is slowly raising the level of the oceans.

ICE AGE OCEANS

Sea levels can rise or fall with changes in climate. At the peak of the last ice age, about 18,000 years ago, the sea level was about 300 feet (91 meters) lower than it is today.

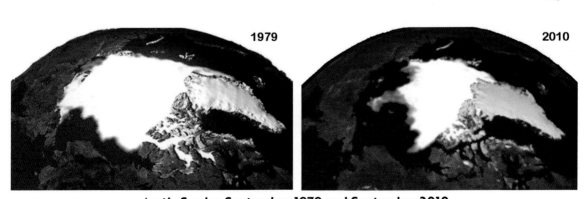

1979

2010

Arctic Sea Ice September 1979 and September 2010

Shrinking Arctic sea ice is a visible sign of a warming climate.

Rising sea levels can cause flooding in coastal cities. Already, nearly a hundred towns and cities along the U.S. East Coast experience regular flooding.

Catastrophic flooding in coastal cities is link climate change.

As the seas rise, people who live in low-lying areas will be at risk.

RISING SEAS

Since 1992, sea levels have risen by about three inches (7.6 centimeters). Scientists predict the oceans will rise between 11 and 38 inches (28 to 97 centimeters) by 2100. This is enough to swamp many cities along the U.S. East Coast.

Anti-flood pumps are a temporary solution for dealing with rising seas.

Coastal flooding in Florida is growing worse.

One of those cities is Miami Beach, Florida. Seawater regularly floods the city's roads, homes, and businesses. So, city leaders are taking action. They are building seawalls to hold back the ocean. They are raising up roads. They are putting in pumps that can remove water after a flood. But this might not be enough. As the seas rise, people in some coastal cities may have no choice but to move.

Farmers are also having to adapt to the effects of climate change. Temperature and rainfall are becoming harder to predict. Severe weather, such as a **drought** or flooding from heavy rains, can kill or damage crops.

New technology can help farmers respond to climate change.

In places where drought already makes farming difficult, climate change presents a serious challenge. But new technologies can help. In Uganda, farmers measure how much rain has fallen and send this information to scientists via mobile phones. Scientists  use the data to predict the upcoming weather. They can let the farmers know how much rain to expect each season. Farmers can then select the best crops to plant. More than 100,000 Ugandan farmers participate in the program.

CHAPTER SIX

YOUR CARBON FOOTPRINT

We all have a carbon footprint. This is the amount of carbon dioxide that is released into the air because of our activities. Your carbon footprint may be big or small, depending on how you live. Some of your activities release carbon dioxide directly. The car or bus you take to school releases carbon dioxide from the tailpipe. Your other activities may release carbon dioxide far away, like the factory that made your blue jeans.

Products made in factories contribute to climate change.

You can take action to shrink your carbon footprint. An easy way is to reduce, reuse, and recycle. Say no to a new phone, or make do with the clothes you already own. Then factories won't burn fossil fuels to make new stuff. Reduce the amount of garbage you throw away. Garbage in a landfill releases methane. This greenhouse gas can warm the atmosphere. Keep stuff out of landfills by **composting** food scraps and lawn waste, and by recycling paper, plastic, metal, and glass.

BUY NOTHING DAY

"Buy Nothing Day" is celebrated on the Friday after Thanksgiving. To participate, just buy nothing that day! It's also a good time to think about your purchases and whether you really need the things you buy.

BURY IT

Gather a few different items from the garbage, such as a paper towel, aluminum foil, egg shells, apple cores, or plastic packaging. Line a cardboard box with a plastic garbage bag. Fill the box partway with soil. Place each item in its own spot on the soil, then cover with more soil. Place the box in a sunny place and keep the soil moist. After two weeks, dig up the samples. What breaks down quickly? What does not? If you like, you can cover the items again and check them in two more weeks.

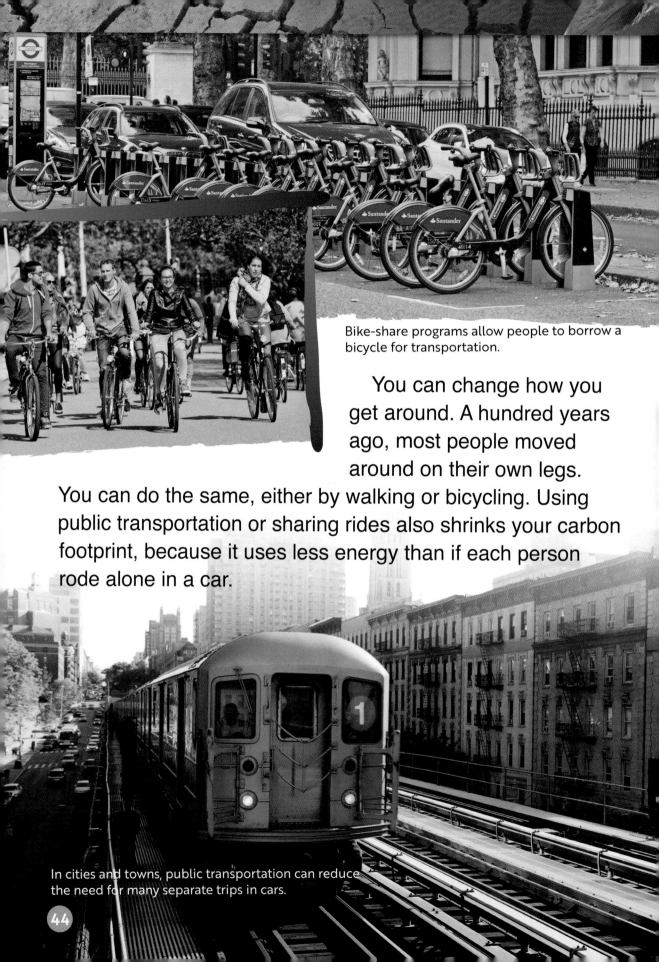

Bike-share programs allow people to borrow a bicycle for transportation.

You can change how you get around. A hundred years ago, most people moved around on their own legs. You can do the same, either by walking or bicycling. Using public transportation or sharing rides also shrinks your carbon footprint, because it uses less energy than if each person rode alone in a car.

In cities and towns, public transportation can reduce the need for many separate trips in cars.

These actions may be small, but they are meaningful. In the end, solving climate change requires all of us to work together. So, speak up. Share your ideas and concerns with others. Talk about climate change with your family, neighbors, and friends. Encourage everyone to be a planet protector.

More and more buildings now come equipped with recycling bins.

Glossary

absorbs (ab-ZORBS): takes in or soaks up through chemical or physical reaction, usually gradually

atmosphere (AT-muh-sfeer): the mass of air surrounding Earth

composting (KAHM-pohst-ing): making compost from decaying plant and animal matter

concentrate (KAHN-suhn-trate): to focus or direct toward a common center

drought (DROUT): a long period of dry weather

emissions (EE-mi-shuhns): substances released into the air

insulate (IN-suh-late): to prevent an object from heating up or cooling down

satellite (SA-tuh-lite): a manmade object or vehicle that is designed to orbit Earth

unreliable (uhn-ree-LEYE-uh-buhl): not reliable, not able to be trusted

vegetation (ve-juh-TAY-shuhn): plants or the rotting remains of plants

Index

Show What You Know

1. How is burning fossil fuels causing Earth to warm?
2. Why are solar power plants often located in deserts?
3. Why might a builder choose local materials for a green building?
4. What items can you recycle to cut your carbon footprint?
5. How do bicycling and walking affect your carbon footprint?

Further Reading

Kamkwamba, Paul, *The Boy Who Harnessed the Wind*, Dial Books, 2015.

Paul, Miranda, *One Plastic Bag: Isatou Ceesay and the Recycling Women of the Gambia*, Millbrook Press, 2015.

Sneideman, Joshua.,*Renewable Energy: Discover the Fuel of the Future With 20 Projects*, Nomad Press, 2016.

About the Author

Rebecca E. Hirsch, Ph.D., earned her doctorate in molecular biology from the University of Wisconsin. She lives in Pennsylvania with her husband and children. She is the author of more than sixty books about science and discovery for children and teens. You can visit her online at www.rebeccahirsch.com.

www.rourkeeducationalmedia.com

PHOTO CREDITS: Credits: www.istock.com, www.shutterstock.com, www.dreamstime.com, Cover: cracked earth vadim kozlovsky, polar bear © vladsilve, solar panels © artjazz, globe courtesy of NASA; Pg4/5; Simon Dannhauer, rottadana, Credit:sakakawea7. Pg6/7; thinkomatic, manjik, francescomoufotografo, tussik13, MattGush. Pg8/9; ByDesignua, NASA, rui_noronha. Pg10/11; imacoconut, Mimadeo, AndreasWeber, ShaunWilkinson. Pg12/13; www.greenleft.org.au, Sbharris-ccBY2.0, NASA, nektofadeev.atgmail.com. 14/15; teaa1946, chart-ccBY2.0. Pg16/17; zstockphotos, tzahiV, Chart-chart-Wiki-ccBY2.0. Pg18/19; Franck-Boston, franckreporter, disqis, BanksPhotos, HildaWeges. Pg20/21; jferrer, qingwa, ebobeldijk, ventdusud. Pg22/23; joel-t, Supersmario, Denis Linine, lazyday, uleiber, Solar Roof Tiles -Tesla, Solar Roof-©Tesla, Patrick_Lauzon. Pg24/25; Pedarilhos, urbanbuzz, viking75, eppicphotography. Pg28/29; Jukkisjupi, lucky-photographer, ufokim. Pg30/31; iChip, Pg32/33; ufokim, saiva, NOAA. 34/34; sumos, dani3315, NOAA. Pg36/37; 3quarks, US Coastguard, monkeybusinessimages. Pg38/39; maxstrz, B137-wiki-cc4, Taglass, Jevtic. Pg40/41; stevanovicigor, mokee81, JerryB7, CherriesJD, paulprescott72, ginosphotos Pg;42/43; JBryson, nikitos77, Sasha_Suzi, KariHoglund. Pg44/45; pjhpix, pjhpix, mizoula, monkeybusinessimages, andyparker72

Edited by: Keli Sipperley

Produced by Blue Door Education for Rourke Educational Media. Cover and Interior design by: Jennifer Dydyk

Planet Protection / Rebecca E. Hirsch
(Taking Earth's Temperature)
  ISBN 978-1-64156-451-9 (hard cover)
  ISBN 978-1-64156-577-6 (soft cover)
  ISBN 978-1-64156-695-7 (e-Book)
Library of Congress Control Number: 2018930478

Rourke Educational Media
Printed in the United States of America, North Mankato, Minnesota